Kafka's Dick

A Comedy £2

Alan Bennett

Samuel French - London
New York - Toronto - Hollywood

CHARACTERS

Kafka
Brod
Linda
Father
Sydney
Hermann K

KAFKA'S DICK

First performed in an earlier version at the Royal Court Theatre, London, on 23rd September, 1986. The cast was as follows:

Kafka	Roger Lloyd Pack
Brod	Andrew Sachs
Linda	Alison Steadman
Father	Charles Lamb
Sydney	Geoffrey Palmer
Hermann K	Jim Broadbent
Julie	Vivian Pickles
Director	Richard Eyre
Designer	William Dudley
Lighting Designer	Mark Henderson
Sound	Christopher Shutt
Music, Effects and Arrangements	George Fenton
Dances	David Toguri

ACT I

The date is immaterial, though it is around 1919

Kafka, a tall, good-looking man is sitting in a chair, dying. Max Brod, his friend, is smaller, slightly hump-backed, and very much alive

Kafka Max.
Brod I hoped you were sleeping.
Kafka Max.

Pause

Brod What?
Kafka I think I shall die soon.

Brod says nothing

Did you hear me, Max?
Brod Let's cross that bridge when you come to it. You've said you were dying before.
Kafka I know. But I won't let you down this time, I promise.
Brod Kafka, I want you to *live*.
Kafka Forgive me. If I die . . .
Brod What's this if? He says he's dying then suddenly it's "if". Don't you mean "when"?
Kafka When I die I want you to do me a favour.
Brod Come to the funeral, you mean? Look, this is Max, your best friend. I'll be up there in the front row.
Kafka No. The funeral can take care of itself.
Brod Pardon me for saying so, but that's typical of your whole attitude to life. A funeral does not take care of itself.
Kafka (*overlapping*) I know, Max. I know.
Brod Take the eats for a start. You're dealing with grief-stricken people. They want to be able to weep secure in the knowledge that once you're in the grave the least they'll be offered will be a choice of sandwiches.
Kafka But after the funeral . . . this is very important . . . I want you to promise me something, Max. You must burn everything I've ever written.
Brod No.
Kafka Stories, novels, letters. Everything.
Brod What about the royalties?
Kafka I've published one novel and a few short stories. Does it matter?
Brod But where would they go in a bereavement situation?

Kafka My father, where else? Which is another reason to burn them. I've got stuff in technical periodicals to do with my work at the insurance company. Don't worry about that ...

Brod But the rest I burn, right?

Kafka Yes.

Brod That is your honest decision?

Kafka Cross my heart and hope to die.

Brod That's not saying much; you are going to die.

Kafka Max, I *mean* it. All my works burned. Understand?

Brod All your works burned.

Kafka Everything. When I go, they go. Finish.

Brod You've got it. Message received and understood.

Pause. Brod starts to go

Kafka Where are you going?

Brod To buy paraffin.

Kafka Max. Stay a minute. After all, my writings are worthless. They wouldn't survive anyway. They don't deserve to survive.

Pause

Don't you think so?

Brod You're the one who's dying. I'm Max, your faithful friend. You say burn them, I burn them. (*Going again*) Maybe I'll get petrol instead.

Kafka Max! (*Pause*) If you want to read them first, feel free ... just to remind you.

Brod (*going again*) No. I read them when you wrote them. I'm going to burn them I may as well press on and burn them. Only ...

Kafka (*brightening*) What?

Brod Well, I ask myself, are we missing an opportunity here? Why not juice up the occasion? ... Ask one or two people over, split a bottle of vino, barbecue the odd steak then as a climax to the proceedings flambé the Collected Works? Anyway, old friend, don't worry. All will be taken care of.

Kafka Good. Still, if in fact you can't get hold of all my stuff, no matter. Some of it has been published. It could be anywhere.

Brod You're kidding. I mean, what are we saying here? This is your faithful friend, Max. Kafka wants his stuff burned, Max will find it and burn it. It won't be difficult. You'd be surprised how helpful people are when it's a dying wish.

Kafka But I'm in libraries, Max. You can't burn them. *Metamorphosis*, my story about a man who wakes up as a beetle. That's in libraries. Ah well. I shall just have to live with that.

Brod Don't be so negative. Here's the plan. I go to the library, borrow your books, go back and say they've been stolen. Then it's burn, baby, burn.

Kafka Some are in America. London. Paris.

Brod So? I've always wanted an excuse to travel. I can't wait. Max Brod. Search and destroy! (*Pause*) Hey, you look really depressed.

Kafka Wouldn't you be depressed? I'm dying.

Pause

Brod Look. *Vis-à-vis* your books. I've just had a thought.

Kafka (*clutching at a straw*) Yes?

Brod Maybe I won't burn everything. Not every single copy. Could you live with that?

Kafka Well ... I ... I'm not sure. I really wanted them burnt ...

Brod Can I just let you in on my thinking? We're in 1920 now, right? You're going to die soon ... give a year, take a year, say 1924 at the outside. Well, less than ten years later we get the Nazis, right? And, as prefigured in some of your as yet unrecognized masterpieces (which I'm going to burn, I know, I know), the Nazis seize power and put into operation the full apparatus of totalitarian bureaucracy.

Kafka Max, I saw it coming.

Brod You did.

Kafka Would that history had proved me wrong, Max.

Brod Would that it had. Only, tragically it didn't. Because in 1933 the Nazis are scheduled to stage their infamous Burning of the Books ...

Kafka Burn books? Who in his right mind would want to burn books? They must be sick.

Brod The Nazis ransack libraries for what they term decadent literature. Film shows Brownshirts bringing out books by the armful and casting them into the flames.

Kafka In civilized Europe! I can't bear it. It's tragic. It's insane. (*Pause*) Max. Which books in particular?

Brod Freud. Proust. Rilke. Brecht.

Kafka Er ... anybody else?

Brod Hemingway. Thomas Mann. Gide. Joyce ...

Kafka Max ... Don't I figure?

Brod Well, this is the point ... I'll have burnt your stuff already.

Kafka But nobody will know that.

Brod Exactly. People will look at the credits and say: They burnt Proust. They burnt Brecht. They burnt Joyce. Where is Kafka? Not worth burning, maybe.

Kafka God. I was depressed before. Now I'm suicidal.

Brod Maybe I can fix it.

Kafka You think?

Brod I can see it now: a shot of flames licking round a book jacket, the name Kafka prominently placed.

Kafka Dreadful.

Brod Sure, but burn one and you sell ten thousand. Believe me, if the Nazis hadn't thought of it the publishers would.

Kafka Max, I'm still not sure. Do I want to survive?

Brod Of course you do. I'm a successful novelist, so I'm headed that way myself. I know you've got talent. You haven't made it big yet, in fact you haven't made it at all, but once you're dead I've a hunch your fame is going to snowball. Who knows, you could end up as famous as me. Whereas, you burn everything, you've squandered your life.

Kafka You're right.

Brod Believe me, in ten years' time, your stuff is going to be classic. That one you mentioned, *Metamorphosis*, where he wakes up one morning and finds he's a cockroach. Brilliant.

Kafka (*leaping from his chair*) That's it. That is *it*. I've changed my mind. As you were. Burn them. Burn everything!

Brod What did I say?

Kafka What did you *say*? What did you say? He didn't wake up as a cockroach. I never said he woke up as a cockroach. He woke up as a beetle.

Brod Cockroach, beetle, they're both bugs, who cares?

Kafka Me! Don't you see? That's the trouble with words. You write one thing, the reader makes it into another. You try to be honest, only words fail you. They always do in the end. They're the worst method of communicating with anybody.

Brod Look . . .

Kafka No, I was right first time. Burn them.

Brod If you say so.

Kafka And Max. No biography.

Brod Who'll want to write your biography? You won't have written anything.

Kafka Promise.

Brod I promise.

Kafka Forgive me. I'm a terrible human being.

Brod Don't worry about it. (*He yawns*)

Kafka I'm just a dog pretending to be a person, an ape.

Brod Yeah, yeah. We've been through all that. Now try and sleep a little. Come to bed.

The Lights begin to fade, with music possibly

Kafka I would sleep, only I dream.

Brod Everybody dreams.

Kafka Not like me. I dream the future.

Kafka and Brod exit

Lights up immediately on:

SCENE 2

The present day. A room in a middle-class house, possibly a kitchen cum living-room. I am not sure how representational the room should be. Since some of the happenings that take place in it are downright unreal perhaps the room should look unreal also, but the reverse could be more convincingly argued. An over-scrupulous naturalism would be out of place, though the reality of the bookcase is crucial. There are doors or exits to other parts of the house, and an entrance, say, french windows on to the garden

Sydney, a mild, middle-aged man, is reading. Linda, his wife, stares out into the garden. Sydney's Father, an old man with a Zimmer frame, is consulting the bookcase

Linda That fool of a tortoise is out again. Galloping across the lawn.
Father When are they coming?
Linda (*ignoring him but without rancour*) They are not coming.
Father (*taking an orange Penguin from the bookcase and carrying it over to Linda*) Is that a detective?
Linda (*still ignoring him*) There are no detectives. Nobody is coming.
Father What have I done?
Sydney (*kindly*) Nothing, Father. You have done nothing. (*Pause*) There can be few people who realize that Hitler went to the same school as Wittgenstein.
Linda The way he went on to behave I'm surprised he went to school at all.
Sydney Another five years they might have been sharing the same desk.
Linda You are clever, Sydney.
Father (*now poised to leave*) When are they coming?
Linda They are not coming.

Father exits

When are they coming?
Sydney They didn't say. (*He looks unhappy*)
Linda Now it's making a beeline for the road. It must want to die.
Sydney I wonder if there was a school magazine. Old Boys' Notes. Wittgenstein, L. (Class of 1904) has just published his *Tractatus Logico-Philosophicus* and been elected a Fellow of Trinity College, Cambridge. Contemporaries will recall the model sewing machine he made out of matchsticks. Hitler, A. (Class of 1899) has recently been elected Chancellor of Germany. He will be remembered as an enthusiastic secretary of the Art Group.
Linda Does Mr Cunliffe read?
Sydney I don't know. As Deputy Supervisor Vehicle Insurance North Western Area I doubt if he gets much chance.

Linda says nothing

I didn't want the job. And remember this: Mr Cunliffe has never had an article in the *Journal of Insurance Studies*.
Linda No, but Mrs Cunliffe's got a new bedroom suite and they pop over to Jersey quite regularly. (*Pause*) Why do you never read novels?
Sydney I'm an insurance man, I prefer facts. Biography. I'd rather read about writers than read what they write.
Linda Yes. I know why. More dirt.
Sydney (*at the bookcase*) Not necessarily. *The Life of E. M. Forster*. Hardly dirt.
Linda Really? I thought he lived with a policeman.
Sydney He was a friend. Forster had friends in many walks of life.

Linda Not merely walks. You said one was an Egyptian tram-driver. And there were umpteen darkies.

Sydney Linda. (*Pause*) We complain about my father: Kafka's father used to rummage in his ears with a toothpick then use it to pick his teeth.

She hangs over his shoulder, looking at his books. She would probably like to be in bed

Linda No pictures?

Sydney No. I sometimes wish biographers carried nude photographs.

Linda Sydney.

Sydney It would settle this argument anyway. (*He holds up a book*) This is by two psychologists at the University of North Carolina, who having analysed everything Kafka ever wrote, deduce that one of his problems, of which there were many, was a small penis.

Linda I never liked the word penis. I don't mind the pee . . . after all that's what it's for. It's the -nis I somehow don't like. Anyway, he's not unique in that department.

Sydney Linda.

Linda I was thinking of Scott Fitzgerald.

Sydney How do you know Scott Fitzgerald had a small . . . thing?

Linda The same way I know W. H. Auden never wore underpants, that Kafka's grandfather could pick up a sack of potatoes in his teeth and that Kafka's father used to rummage in his ears with a toothpick. Because that kind of conversation is all I ever get. If it weren't for looking after your father I could still be a nurse.

Sydney I like odd facts.

Linda When are you going to tell me the bits in between? I'd thought of taking a course. So I can help you in your work.

Sydney An insurance course?

Linda This work.

Sydney If there are courses in Kafka, which I doubt, they would be the first casualty of the cutbacks.

Linda Literature in general.

Sydney Ah. Literature in general.

Linda I should have stayed a nurse. What do I do now? Hang about. I'm nothing.

Sydney I know it's a wicked thing to say nowadays but you are not nothing. You are my wife.

Linda It's not enough.

Sydney It's enough for Mrs Cunliffe.

Linda Couldn't I do research? File your papers?

She makes a move to do so. He stops her

Sydney Linda.

Linda Let me at least read it.

Sydney (*taking back his manuscript*) You wouldn't understand it.

Linda I might. After all he's got a nice face. Would I have liked him?

Sydney He was never short of symptoms. You could at least have nursed him. You wouldn't like his stories. Not what you'd call "true to life". A man turns into a cockroach. An ape lectures. Mice talk. He'd like me. We've got so much in common. He was in insurance. I'm in insurance. He had TB. I had TB. He didn't like his name. I don't like my name. I'm sure the only reason I drifted into insurance was because I was called Sydney.

Linda Sydney's a nice name. I like Sydney.

Sydney Now this is interesting. Kafka had read *Crime and Punishment*, which is a novel by Dostoevsky. In *Crime and Punishment* the student Raskolnikov commits a murder for which another man is wrongly arrested; the man is a house painter. In Kafka's *The Trial*, Joseph K is wrongly arrested. Who has actually committed the crime? A house painter. And someone in whose name millions of people were wrongly arrested was Adolf Hitler. Who is himself wrongly accused of being . . . a house painter.

Pause

Linda And?

Sydney Linda, it's interesting.

Linda It is, it is.

Sydney One of the functions of literary criticism is to point up unexpected connections.

Linda With you being in accident insurance I thought your only interest in unexpected connections was when they occurred between motor cars. Sydney.

She draws him out of the chair

Sydney Linda. It's two-thirty in the afternoon.

Linda It'll be another unexpected connection.

The doorbell goes. They stop

Sydney Is his case packed?

Linda nods

Linda (*meaning "Be brave"*) Sydney.

Linda answers the door, but the visitor has already come round to the french windows. It is Brod, who is just as we have seen him previously, except that he is minus his hump. He carries in his hand a large Homburg hat which conceals a tortoise

Brod I ring your doorbell with reluctance. I have met with an accident. I am a visitor to these shores. Suddenly a temperamental prostate and a total absence of toilet facilities necessitates my emptying my bladder outside your front door.

Linda returns

Linda Sydney, it's all over the step.

Brod Worse is to follow. Picture my distress as I am rebuttoning my trousers when I discover I have urinated not only over your doorstep but also over your tortoise. (*He removes the Homburg to reveal the tortoise*)

Linda Our tortoise? (*She puts out her hand for the tortoise then thinks better of it*) He's wet through!

Brod puts the tortoise down on the floor. It begins to move off—Brod, without looking, puts his Homburg hat over it

Sydney It was an accident, I'm sure.

Brod Blame the disappearance of your public conveniences. Time was they were the envy of the civilized world. To be incontinent here is some problem, I can tell you.

The doorbell has alerted Father and he has come in

Father It's not true. Someone's been telling lies about me. I am not incontinent. Furthermore I can tell you the name of the Prime Minister. Are you them?

Sydney No, he is not them. There is no them. This gentleman has just urinated over the tortoise.

Father I know what that means. You want my room.

Brod Why does urinating over the tortoise mean they want your room?

Sydney My father imagines things.

Father I don't imagine things. You say I imagine things. I never imagine things.

At which point Brod's hat begins to move slowly across the room towards Father, who retreats before it in shocked silence, then (Zimmer frame permitting) bolts

Linda picks up the hat and hands it to Brod. Ignoring the cue to go he sits down and opens a book

Sydney Should we offer him a cup of tea?

Linda And put another innocent tortoise at risk? No.

Brod How singular! I open a book and what do I find? Kafka. (*Opening others*) Kafka, Kafka.

Sydney You know his work?

Brod Only by heart. "As Gregor Samsa awoke one morning from uneasy dreams he found himself transformed into a gigantic cockroach." "Ah, ha," says the browser at the airport bookstall. "The very thing to while away my flight to Sri Lanka." And ring a ding ding. It's another sale for our Czech Chekhov.

Linda I was a nurse. Waking up people was half my job. I never came across anyone waking up as an insect.

Brod You probably never came across metaphor either. She says no-one wakes up as a cockroach. Next to her I'd wake up a wild beast. So what is it about our Prague Proust that interests you?

Sydney It's not generally known but Kafka worked all his life in an insurance office . . .

Brod It is known to some people.

Sydney And as I'm in that line myself, I'm writing a piece about him for *Small Print*, the *Journal of Insurance Studies*.

Brod For a moment I thought you were yet another of those academic blow flies who make a living buzzing round the faeces of the famous. You've read his biography?

Sydney I've read several.

Brod Excuse me. There is only one. Mine.

Sydney You've written a biography of Kafka?

Brod I wrote the biography. I edited the diaries. I published the novels. You want to know about Kafka, start here. Max Brod.

They shake hands

Sydney Max Brod! You are Max Brod? You're pulling my leg. No. (*He laughs nervously*) How could you be?

Brod Why?

Sydney You're Kafka's closest friend.

Brod Correction. Not his closest friend. His only friend. His only real friend.

Sydney You're a great man. A legend. What would you be doing here? Max Brod! (*He shakes hands again*)

Brod What about Nurse Cavell? Doesn't she want to shake hands with a legend?

Linda Brod? You spell it B–R–O–D? (*She goes to look it up*)

Sydney No need to look him up. I know all about him.

Brod (*to the audience*) She's about to discover I'm dead. But then I'm also famous. These are the dead ones. Nobody's ever heard of them. That's death. You read my book?

Sydney Every word.

Linda (*beckoning him with the book*) Sydney.

Sydney I've read half a dozen biographies but I always come back to yours.

Brod Of course you do. I knew Kafka. They didn't.

Linda Sydney, can I have a word?

Sydney In a minute, Linda. Tell me, was Kafka as saintly as you make him out?

Brod's interest throughout this conversation is in Linda, not Kafka and still less Sydney

Brod I should lie? Kind, modest and with that clod of a father . . . what type of a nurse was this, crisp, white uniform, thin, black stockings . . . that type?

Linda Yes. Strict. And I was a past master of the enema. Sydney.

Sydney (*eluding Linda's attempts to draw him aside*) To me Kafka is the last, authentic, modern saint. It's interesting that one by one the moral giants of the twentieth century have all been toppled. I say that in my article. "It is interesting that one by one the moral giants of the twentieth century have all been toppled." But not Kafka.

Brod That's fascinating. Nurses have a reputation for unbridled promiscuity. How does that accord with your experience?

Linda Sydney.

Sydney Take Wittgenstein. People said he was a saint, but not any more.

Linda (*feigning interest*) No?

Sydney Biography reveals that his less philosophical moments were spent picking up youths.

Brod What for, when there's so much else on offer?

Sydney And who nowadays admires Freud?

Linda Oh? Where did he slip up?

Sydney Dishonest. Freud was quite small . . .

Brod Minute. He would only have come up to here (*on Linda*).

Sydney And yet in a photograph of Freud with his colleagues he's head and shoulders above everybody else. Why? Biography reveals he's stood on a box.

Linda Oh. Like Alan Ladd.

Sydney Alan Ladd?

Linda Alan Ladd wasn't tall. He often had to stand on a box. Either that or his leading lady stood in a trench. Maybe Freud wasn't on a box. Maybe the others were in a trench.

Sydney Linda. Nursing, though an admirable profession, doesn't exactly hone the mind.

Brod Don't worry about it.

Linda But Sydney. You said literary criticism was about unexpected connections. You can't get more unexpected than Freud and Alan Ladd.

Brod That's the danger with big tits. The mind goes on holiday.

Linda Sydney, I want to tell you something.

Sydney Linda, I'm talking. You wouldn't catch Kafka standing on a box. Wanting to make himself bigger. Not your friend Kafka, eh?

Brod No.

Sydney In fact, I'd have said the reverse. I'd have said he wanted to make himself smaller. Would you agree?

Brod Larger, smaller, one or the other. You don't still have your uniform?

Linda Where's the tortoise gone?

She gets down on her hands and knees to look, further fascinating Brod

Sydney We only have to look at his work. Who does Kafka identify with? An ape, a mouse, a cockroach. Smaller and smaller.

Brod Can I help?

Sydney I tell you, give him a few more years and he'd have needed a microscope to see what he was writing about. I actually say that in my article: "Give him a few more years and he'd have needed a microscope to see what he was writing about."

Brod How interesting. Will it ever stop? If I never hear the name Kafka again it will be too soon. (*He sits down again*)

Linda Sydney. You don't think he is this man?

Sydney I'm not sure. Max Brod was a hunchback.

Linda Sydney. He's also dead. I looked him up for you. (*She shows him the book*) Died in 1968.

Sydney In Tel Aviv, yes.

Linda You know?

Sydney Of course.

Linda So who is he?

Sydney He could be to do with father. A health visitor perhaps.

Linda Masquerading as a friend of Kafka?

Sydney The social services are notorious for their imagination.

Linda So why not ask him?

Sydney Linda. Don't *worry*. We are having a conversation. Ideas are being exchanged, hypotheses put forward. For me this is a treat. A picnic of the mind. How often do I find someone who's even heard of Kafka let alone someone who can't wait to discuss him?

Linda Yes, Sydney.

Sydney All in good time.

Linda Yes, Sydney.

Sydney (*finding the tortoise*) Here he is. Why don't you put him under the tap?

Linda I'll go put him under the tap.

Brod Can I help?

Linda No. You stay and have a picnic with my husband.

She exits

Sydney There's one question I must ask you.

Brod I won't answer it.

Sydney You don't know the question.

Brod I don't know the question? I don't know the question? There is only one question. Always there has been just one question. "Why did you not burn the papers?" Nobody, *nobody* is grateful. But for me there would have been no Kafka. He would not have existed. He would have been a no-name. A big zero. I made Kafka. Me! Max Brod. So is it "Thank you, Max", "Much obliged, Max", "Good thinking, Max"? No. Always it's "Why did you not burn the papers?" Well, there is one person who would thank me. The man himself. If Kafka were around today he'd be the first person to shake my hand.

There is a shrill scream from Linda, off

Kafka appears on the stage beside Brod

Linda (*off*) Sydney! Sydney!

Brod You!

Kafka takes his hand as:

Linda enters

Linda It's that tortoise. I'd swilled it under the tap and put it on the draining board. Just then it popped its little head out ... I don't know what made me do it ... I gave it a kiss.

Brod Kafka.

Sydney Kafka? Linda. I believe this is Kafka. It is. It is. Linda. This is
  Kafka.
Linda Sydney.
Kafka How are you?
Brod Good. Terrific. You?
Kafka Terrible.

They laugh

Brod You haven't changed.
Kafka (*embracing him*) Max, Max. Old friend.
Sydney (*shyly*) How do you do.
Kafka (*taking Linda's hand*) How do you do.
Linda (*panicking*) Sydney.
Sydney Have I the pleasure of addressing Mr Kafka?

Kafka nods graciously and diffidently shakes hands

  I just don't believe it. Kafka!
Kafka Max. Who is this man?
Sydney Linda. It's him. It's Kafka.
Linda Sydney. Kafka's dead. They're both dead.
Sydney I know. But it's Kafka.
Linda Sydney.
Kafka Max. Kindly ask him not to keep saying my name. You remember I
  never liked my name. The persistent repetition of it is still deeply
  offensive.
Brod Sure. I remember. Listen, boys and girls. Kafka doesn't like his name.
  Point taken. No more Kafka. (*To Kafka*) The husband's very dull but the
  wife has possibilities.
Sydney I love you. You're my hero.
Kafka Hero? Max, what is this?
Linda Excuse me. I hope I'm not out of order but two minutes ago you were
  a tortoise. Suddenly you're a leading light in European literature.
Brod My dear Miss Marple. This is someone who wrote a story about a
  man waking up as a cockroach. So? Now it's a two-way traffic.
Linda That was fiction. Wasn't it, Sydney? This is non-fiction.
Kafka (*to the audience*) What is this about a leading figure in European
  literature?
Sydney Kafka at 27 Batcliffe Drive!
Kafka Max. Is this man deaf? He is still saying my name.
Brod Please. Please. This is the second time of asking. Drop Kafka's name.

Sydney and Linda draw aside

Kafka What is all this "leading figure in European literature" stuff?
Brod Well?
Kafka I'm nobody. I brought out a few short stories and an unsuccessful
  novel—that was seventy years ago in Czechoslovakia. How am I a leading
  figure?
Brod Did I say modest? Move over E. M. Forster. A saint.

Kafka And Max. A beetle.

Brod Say again.

Kafka Not a cockroach. You said cockroach. It was a beetle.

Brod Will you listen to this man. I make him world famous and he quibbles over entomology.

Brod and Kafka draw aside

Linda Call the police.

Sydney What for? Nobody's committed a crime.

Linda Sydney. It's a Tuesday afternoon. We're expecting someone from the Health Authority and meanwhile you're kicking around some thoughts about Kafka. A knock on the door and it's a stranger with a dripping wet tortoise in his hand, who, lo and behold, turns out to be the world's leading authority on Kafka. Notwithstanding this person seems to have died several years ago you engage him in conversation while I go and swill the tortoise. The next minute it's gone, we've got Kafka in the lounge and these two are falling into one another's arms.

Sydney Well?

Linda It just seems a bit too plausible to me.

Sydney So who are they?

Linda Burglars.

Sydney Don't be absurd. How many burglars have heard of Franz Kafka?

Linda Sydney, they read all sorts in prison. They no sooner get them inside nowadays than they're pestering them to read Proust. That's all some of them go to prison for, the chance of a good read.

Sydney It would have to be a subtle burglar who got in disguised as a tortoise. It's not logical.

Linda Criminals have no logic. A woman last week answers the door, the caller shoves a dishcloth in her mouth and steals the television set. You say he couldn't be a tortoise, she's now a vegetable, so don't talk to me about logic. Call the police. Let them decide if he's Kafka.

Sydney What with? Sniffer dogs trained in Modern Studies?

Linda Sydney, he's dead. They're both dead.

Sydney They're alive to me. Franz Kafka is more present, more real to me than . . . than . . .

Linda I know. Than I am.

Sydney When do we ever talk, Linda?

Linda Sydney, we're always talking.

Sydney Not about ideas, Linda. About candlewick bedspreads. The electricity bill. Your mother's eczema. That's what you talk about.

Linda I do not. Mother's eczema cleared up last week. I told you, she got some new ointment. And I know I don't talk about candlewick bedspreads because they went out years ago. That's why we should get rid of ours. We want a continental quilt. (*Pause*) We could afford one. The electric bill's quite reasonable. All right. I'm not clever. Why do you think I want to learn? Only you won't teach me. So I'm boring.

Sydney Linda . . .

Linda But if it's a choice between boredom and burglary I'm calling the police.

She goes off with Sydney in hot pursuit

Kafka I just think it's odd her calling me a leading figure in European literature.

Brod It is odd. (*Aside*) Wait till I tell him he's world famous, the author of several major masterpieces.

Kafka He seemed to think I was somebody too.

Brod This is England. It doesn't take much to be a celebrity here. (*Aside*) He is going to be over the *moon*.

Kafka I published so little and you destroyed the rest.

Brod (*aside*) Good job I didn't.

Kafka You did, didn't you?

Brod Of course. It was your last wish.

Kafka Dear, faithful Max.

Brod Though say I hadn't burned it all. And say . . . it's ridiculous of course . . . but say you turned out to be quite famous. You wouldn't mind?

Kafka Mind? No. I wouldn't mind. It's just that I'd never forgive you.

Brod But I'm your best friend.

Kafka So it's worse. You'd have betrayed me. No. That would be it between us. Over. Finish. Still, what are we talking about? You burned them. I'm not famous. Everybody's happy.

Brod Happy? I'm ruined.

Linda returns with Sydney in hot pursuit, Linda bent on confronting Kafka

Sydney You know nothing about this.

Linda I just want to find out exactly who they are.

Sydney Linda.

Linda Can I ask you some questions?

Kafka Of course.

Sydney She means about your work.

Linda I mean about you.

Brod His work. She mustn't ask him about his work. Oh, my God.

Kafka Feel free. Ask any question you like.

Brod I'm sorry. Sorry. I don't want any questions. Kafka does not want questions.

Kafka What about my work?

Brod What about his work? There is no work. I burnt all the work.

Kafka I don't mind talking about my work.

Brod Exactly. Who are these people anyway? . . . You don't?

Kafka Why should I? I worked in an insurance office.

Brod What am I talking about? Of course you did. Kafka worked in an insurance office. Tell us about it. It sounds fascinating.

Linda Sydney works in insurance too.

Brod Really? How boring.

Sydney I didn't mean that work I meant your real work.

Brod What is this, some kind of interrogation? (*Recovering himself*) I have
to tell you, this is a shy man.

Kafka Max, I'm not. He always thought I was shy. I wasn't. I even went to
a nudist colony.

Linda That is brave.

Brod Not if you don't take your trunks off.

Sydney Excuse my asking, but why didn't you take your trunks off? Had
you something to hide?

Kafka Yes. *No.*

Sydney I have this theory that biographies would benefit from a photograph of the subject naked.

Kafka Naked? What a terrible idea.

Brod Shocking. And who, pray, is talking about biography. *No-one.* No-
one at all. In the meantime, old friend, let's recall why you went to that
nudist camp in the first place. You were delicate. You had a bad chest,
remember. So why don't you just step out into the garden and fill what's
left of your lungs with some fresh air.

Kafka Max. It is raining.

Brod Here is an umbrella.

Kafka Max!

But he goes, bundled out into the garden by Brod

Linda I'm calling the police now, while he's in the garden.

She exits

Sydney (*ready to go after her*) Why? They can't arrest him. He's committed
no crime.

Brod Calm down. He wrote the script for that one. (*He sits down*) Cigar?

Sydney I don't smoke.

Brod Neither do I. Look . . .

Sydney Sydney.

Brod Syd. There's been a small misunderstanding. Nothing of importance.
You recall how at one point in his life Kafka intimated I might consider
burning his writings?

Sydney On his deathbed, yes.

Brod (*furious again*) It was not his deathbed. It was prior to his deathbed.
He was around for years after that. (*To the audience*) Blood and sand,
why does everybody round here think they're an authority on Kafka? He
thinks he knows about Kafka. *Kafka* thinks he knows about Kafka. I'm
the only one who really knows.

Sydney What is he doing in the garden?

Brod God knows. Giving the kiss of life to an ant, probably. Why wasn't I a
friend of Ernest Hemingway? Where are you going?

Sydney I've some questions I want to ask him . . .

Brod No, look . . .

Sydney Sydney.

Brod OK, Syd. I didn't burn the papers . . .

Sydney (*trying to go out into the garden again*) That's one of my questions.
Does he mind?

Brod *Syd.* No! Of course he doesn't mind. Why should he mind? Still if it's
all the same to you I'd rather you . . . deferred the question a while.

Sydney Why?

Brod Why? Yes, why? Because . . . because he doesn't know.

Sydney He doesn't know what?

Brod He doesn't know I didn't burn the papers.

Sydney He doesn't know you didn't burn the papers!

Brod So what? He is not going to mind.

Sydney No?

Brod No. Why should he?

Sydney Why should he? That's right. As you say in your book, this is a
saint.

Brod Sure, sure.

Sydney He'll forgive you.

Brod Nothing to forgive.

Sydney In fact he'll be pleased.

Brod Pleased? He'll be ecstatic.

Sydney I would be. Can I be the one to tell him? I'd like that.

Brod No. Not yet.

Sydney When?

Brod When? Well, I think we've got to be very careful about this. Choose
the moment. And while we're on the subject, less of this "leading figure in
European literature" stuff.

Sydney Why?

Brod Because, dummy, if I had burnt his papers he wouldn't be, would he?

Sydney No I suppose he wouldn't. What you're saying is he doesn't know
he's Kafka.

Brod He knows he's Kafka. He doesn't know he's *Kafka.*

Sydney Mmm. It's a tricky one.

Brod Why don't we play a game? He thinks he has no reputation at all.
Let's pretend he *has* no reputation at all. Then come the right moment
Max here will spill the beans and we can all have a big laugh.

Sydney Yes. A big laugh, yes. Ha ha.

Brod Where is the bathroom?

Sydney Follow me. Wouldn't that be a lie?

Brod Listen, Syd. I am Max Brod. I was short-listed for the Nobel Prize.
Don't tell me about lies. Here he comes.

Sydney Wait. Let me get this right. The game is: I don't know him, I've
never heard of him.

Brod Right.

Sydney Though when you do get round to telling him, I'd like him to
autograph his books.

Brod Weidenfeld and Nicolson! His books! We've got to get rid of his
books.

Brod rushes to the bookcase and starts removing books as:

Kafka comes in

Kafka Books?

Brod Yes. Well, no. You could call them books. They're dirty books. Pornography. Smut.

Sydney looks hurt, and opens his mouth to protest but thinks better of it

Kafka How despicable. His poor wife. I remember I once said "A book should be like an axe to break up the frozen seas within us."

Brod joins in to finish the quotation

Brod Well, these are some of the ones that failed the test.

Sydney is helping to shift the books outside also. Sydney often has to retrieve books right from under Kafka's nose

Kafka Excuse me. I—I thought I saw my name.

Sydney Your name? Sorry ... (*Winking at Brod*) What was your name again?

Kafka Kafka. Franz Kafka.

Sydney No, no. This is the Hollywood movie director. Frank Capra.

Kafka (*wistfully, looking at the bookshelves*) It's like looking for one's headstone in a cemetery.

Brod is carrying another pile of books out when Sydney bumps into him and the books go all over the floor

What's that?

Sydney What?

Kafka That one. It says *Kafka's Novels*.

Sydney This? *Kafka's Novels*? No. *Tarzan's Navel*.

Brod (*quickly taking it*) Anthropology.

Kafka And that one. *The Loneliness of Kafka*.

Sydney *The Loneliness of Kafka*? No. *The Loneliness of Raffia*. As an adjunct to her nursing course my wife did occupational therapy. Hence this one: *Raffia: The Debate Continues*. *The Agony of Raffia*, the endless plaiting, the needle going in and out, suddenly the needle slips, ah! Few people realize the single-minded devotion that goes into the humble table mat.

By this time Sydney thinks he has gathered up all the fallen books. However, one has eluded him. Sydney and Brod are transfixed with horror as Kafka picks it up

Kafka Proust.

They sigh with relief

Sydney Great man. A genius.

Kafka You think?

Brod Listen. A bit more get up and go and you'd have run rings round him.

Kafka I was ill. I had a bad chest.

Sydney Proust had a worse chest than you.

Kafka How does he know about my chest?

Brod He doesn't. (Fool!) Anyway, what is this, the TB Olympics?

Kafka (*reading Proust*) "For a long time I used to go to bed early." For a long time I scarcely went to bed at all.

Sydney Yes, only Proust wrote a major novel. What did you do? Sorry, what *is* your name again?

Brod (*aside*) Don't overdo it.

Sydney Then *hurry*.

Kafka (*to Max*) Who is this Proust?

Sydney Who is this Proust? *Who is this Proust?* Beg pardon. Only the greatest writer of the twentieth century.

Kafka (*meaning "protect me against this terrible information"*) Max.

Sydney (*playing for time while Brod clears the books*) Proust is a lifelong invalid and sufferer from asthma. Lesser men this would stop. *Oui.* Does it stop Proust? *Non.* He lives on a noisy street, the noisiest street in Paris. So, does he sit back and say "It's too noisy. I can't write here" *"Il y a beaucoup de bruit. Je ne peux pas écrire ici"*? Not at all.

Brod *Pas du tout.*

Sydney *Eh bien*, what does he do?

Brod *Qu'est ce qu'il fait?*

Sydney *Le voilà.* He builds himself a cork-lined room . . . *une chambre* (*looking to Brod for the translation*) . . .

Brod (*lamely*) Cork-lined.

Sydney And in this room . . . (*showing signs of weariness by now*) *dans cette chambre . . . il . . .*

Kafka Oh shut up. Max. My room was noisy. It was next door to my parents. When I was trying to write I had to listen to them having sexual intercourse. I'm the one who needed the cork-lined room. And he's the greatest writer of the twentieth century. Oh God.

Brod Listen. More than Proust ever wrote you burned. Or I burned . . .

Brod thinks he has cleared the books when Linda returns with a pile

Linda Sydney. These don't belong in the hall.

Brod Oh my God!

Linda What's the matter with the bookcase?

Sydney Full. Chock-a-block.

Linda There's tons of room.

Kafka (*helping*) Allow me.

Linda Thank you.

Sydney No. (*Seizing the books*) I'm—I'm throwing them out.

Linda What for?

Sydney (*nonplussed*) What for?

Brod He's—he's selling them to me.

Linda (*seizing the books back*) The penny drops. I've heard about people like you. Insinuating yourself into people's homes. Sydney. This is how mother lost her gate-legged table.

A book falls. Kafka stoops for it, but Brod is there first

Brod Give me that.

Linda Look. He can't wait to get his hands on them.
Sydney Linda, (*seizing the books again*) I just want them outside.
Linda Why?
Sydney (*desperately to Brod*) Why?
Brod I need to go to the toilet. Now.
Sydney Well, for God's sake don't do it over the goldfish or else we'll be
entertaining the Brontë sisters.

*He rushes out after Brod carrying the books, leaving Kafka and Linda alone
for the first time*

Kafka You think I'm a criminal?
Linda I think your friend is.
Kafka Perhaps you should think of me as a dream.
Linda I've rung the police.
Kafka The police also have dreams.
Linda They didn't think you were from the Health Authority.
Kafka That's not surprising. I never had much to do with either Health or
Authority. The only authority I had came from sickness. TB.
Linda Sydney had TB. That's how we met. They can cure it now.
Kafka I'm sure people find other things to die of.
Linda If they take that attitude they probably do.
Kafka You sound like a girl I used to know.

Linda sits down and crosses her legs

I say, that's good.
Linda What?
Kafka The way you took one of your legs and just flung it over the other.
You've done it again. Perfect.
Linda Don't be silly. Everybody can do that.
Kafka No.
Linda I just don't think about it.
Kafka But in order not to think about it one has to give it a good deal of
thought.

Linda tries again and muffs it

Linda It's a simple thing. Like walking.
Kafka Is walking simple? Stand up.

Linda stands up

You are going to cross the room. For a start you must decide which leg
you're going to move first. Have you come to a decision? Wait. Remember when you're moving whichever leg it is you've decided to move first
you should meanwhile be thinking about the one you're going to move
after that. Slowly. Oh, you've chosen that leg. I see. Now the other leg.
Now the first leg. Now the same leg as you used the time before last. And
now this one again, which is the one you used the time before that.

*Linda starts to laugh and stagger and, pealing with laughter, falls into
Kafka's arms*

At which point Brod and Sydney enter

Sydney Linda.

Linda He was just teaching me how to walk.

Sydney Oh. I thought you'd just about got that licked.

Brod Can I help?

Linda Don't touch me.

Brod It's always the same. As soon as they meet him it's good-night Max.

Linda How slim you are.

Kafka I know. Forgive me.

Sydney Odd when one remembers what a big man your father was.

Kafka A giant ... how did you know that?

Sydney Er, he told me. Didn't you?

Brod Did I? Of course I did. "What a big man his father was", I remember saying. This isn't a game.

Sydney I thought you said it was.

Brod What about her? She won't give us away.

Sydney No. She's not an intellectual. This is just an ex-nurse. Say Heidegger to her and she thinks it's a lager.

Linda Sydney has a father too.

Kafka It's not uncommon.

Linda Only he doesn't pick his ears with a toothpick.

Kafka My father used to do that.

Linda I know.

Kafka How?

Sydney I told her.

Brod And I told him.

Kafka You say this Proust is well thought of?

Brod Not by me. It's a sick mind.

Linda He liked boys.

Kafka (*shocked*) Boys?

Linda I know. Some men do. Wittgenstein did. Whoever he was.

Brod Not an intellectual? This is Susan Sontag! What does it matter? Nobody blames them. They're dead. Death does that for writers. "Death is to the individual like Saturday evening is to the chimneysweep: it washes the dirt from his body."

Kafka That's not bad, Max. I'd like to have said that.

Brod You did Kafka, you did. It was one of the things I burnt.

Kafka I was better than I thought.

Brod You were.

Kafka What a pity.

Sydney (*nudging Brod*) Go on. Now.

Brod There's something I have to tell you.

Sydney I can't wait for this.

Linda What?

Brod It's about burning your books.

Sydney Here it comes.

Kafka No need to tell me, old friend. I know.

Brod You know?

Kafka I know.

Brod (*to Sydney*) He knows.
Sydney (*to Linda*) He knows.
Linda Knows what?
Brod And ... you don't blame me?
Kafka Why should I blame you? How could I?
Brod Will you listen to this man. Did I say a saint? Shake hands with a saint. He knows.
Linda What do you know?
Kafka Once upon a time I asked my friend here to destroy all my writings. I know that he feels bad because he obeyed me.
Brod He doesn't know.
Kafka Don't *worry*. I sometimes feel the same. But what's done is done.
Brod I'm going to have to try a different tack.
Sydney You are.
Linda Sydney ...
Sydney Be quiet.
Brod Old friend, from that distinguished bundle which I so dutifully thrust into the incinerator I'd like to recall a particularly choice example of what perished that day: "Somebody must have been telling lies about Joseph K——"
Brod ⎫ (*together*) ⎧ "—because one fine morning he woke up and found
Kafka ⎭   ⎩ himself under arrest."
Kafka I remember. Two mysterious men arrive to arrest Joseph K who doesn't know what offence he has committed. Then he has to appear before a tribunal somewhere.
Brod And to get to the courtroom he has to go through somebody's kitchen——
Linda Really? (*She glances round her kitchen*)
Kafka —where people just seemed to take him for granted. He never does find out what he's done.
Brod And in the end he's executed.
Kafka Did I ever give that one a title?
Brod A great title: *The Trial* by Franz Kafka.
Kafka That doesn't make it sound like a detective story?
Sydney The public like detective stories.
Brod Only what have we got instead? A short story about a guy who wakes up as a cockroach.
Kafka A beetle, Max. A beetle. Why can you never get it right?
Brod Listen, for all the good you would have done for yourself he could have woken up a fucking centipede.
Kafka Max!
Linda One more off-colour remark and he'll have to leave, won't he, Sydney? Won't he?

Father has entered in his overcoat with a little attaché case. He is carrying the orange Penguin book he took in the beginning. He catches Linda's last phrase and assumes it was meant for him

Father Leave? Well, I'm ready. Somebody's been telling lies about me. They've come to take me away and I don't know what I've done.

Sydney Sit down, Father.

Linda I'll get him a tablet. Father thinks we're going to put him in a home.

Kafka And are you?

Linda We didn't want to. But he's driven us so mad asking when we decided in the end we'd better.

Kafka I sympathize. I hated my father. I once wrote him a letter telling him so. Why one can't just get rid of parents I don't understand. One puts the cat out when it's a nuisance, why not them?

Sydney Your father was different.

Kafka How do you know?

Brod How many more times? Because I told him.

Brod exits to the garden. Linda exits for a tablet

Sydney Listen, Father. They won't take you away if you can answer some simple questions. The day of the week.

Father Yes. I've got that off by heart.

Sydney The name of the Prime Minister.

Father Yes.

Sydney And some simple sums. Hang on to those and you'll be all right.

Kafka In youth we take examinations to get into institutions. In old age to keep out of them.

Father (*putting the Penguin down*) You said this was a detective. It's not a detective at all.

Linda returns with the tablet

Linda There are no detectives.

Sydney assists Linda as she takes Father out

You have a beautiful Portuguese rug in your room. I can't think why you want to keep coming down here.

Kafka is alone on the stage. He picks up the Penguin and looks at it idly. Then less idly

Kafka (*reading aloud the first sentence*) "Somebody must have been telling lies about Joseph K because one fine morning he was arrested . . ." (*He turns the book over to look at the title. There is a moment of shocked silence, then shouting*) MAX!

Nobody comes

Kafka rushes off and comes back with some of the books taken off the bookshelf

(*Looking at them and throwing them down as he comes*) Kafka! Kafka! Kafka! Novels, stories, letters.

Brod creeps on

Brod (*faintly*) Sorry.
Kafka Sorry? SORRY? Max. You publish everything I ever wrote and you're *sorry*! I trusted you.
Brod You exaggerated. You always did.
Kafka So, I say burn them, what do you think I mean, *warm* them?
Brod I thought it was just false modesty.
Kafka All modesty is false, otherwise it's not modesty. There must be every word here that I've ever written.

Linda comes in

Linda What did he do?
Kafka It's not what he did. (*Indicating the books*) It's what he didn't do. *This is* what he did.

Sydney comes in with a further pile of books

Did I write these too? Oh my God!
Sydney No. These are some of the books about you. Only a few. I believe the Library of Congress catalogue lists some fifteen thousand.
Kafka Max. What have you done to me?
Brod Ask not what I've done to you, but what you've done for humanity. You, who never knew you were a great man, now rank with Flaubert, Tolstoy and Dostoevsky, called fellow by the greatest names in literature. As Shakespeare spoke for mankind on the threshold of the modern world you speak mankind's farewell in the authentic voice of the twentieth century.
Kafka (*in a small, awe-stricken voice*) Shit.
Sydney He's taking it very badly.
Brod Don't worry. He'll be all over me in a minute. But who else would treat fame like this, eh? Chekhov? He'd be round to the estate agents, looking at a little place in the country with paddock and mature fruit trees attached. Zola would be installing a jacuzzi. Even T. S Eliot'd have people round for drinks. But what does Kafka do?
Sydney Finds the whole thing a trial.
Brod Exactly. The humility of the man. I tell you, if I were Jesus Christ I'd be looking over my shoulder.
Kafka Judas!
Brod He's made you one of the biggest names in twentieth-century literature.
Linda Even I've heard of you.
Kafka (*with exaggerated patience*) I didn't want a big name. I wanted a small name. I shrank my name. I pared it down to nothing. I'd have been happy with no name at all.
Sydney But that's the secret of your success. You've got a name for anonymity. *The Trial*: a nameless man's search for justice in a faceless bureaucracy. When Eastern Europe went communist this was the book that told you about it before it happened. In so many words . . .
Kafka That's it. That's it. So many words. I've added so many words to the world I've made it heavier.

Brod Some day you'll thank me.

Kafka Max, this is some day.

Brod is going to speak

I don't want to speak to you. If you want to talk to somebody talk to Kafka.

Sydney But you are Kafka.

Kafka No, I'm not. Kafka is a vast building; a ramshackle institution in every room and department of which, in every corridor, attic and cellar, students and scholars pore over my text and worry over my work. That isn't me. That is Kafka. Communicate with that. Preferably in triplicate.

Sydney This piece I'm writing about you for the *Journal of Insurance Studies* . . .

Kafka Don't talk to me about it. He's the expert.

Sydney No, but . . .

Kafka Please.

An awkward silence in which Brod and Sydney are at one side of the stage, Kafka and Linda at the other

Linda When did you first get the writing bug then?

Kafka I'd rather not talk about it.

Linda I have to confess, I've never read a word you've written.

Kafka Good.

Sydney Wouldn't understand it if she did.

Linda I might. How would you know? You never talk to me. I know tons of things about literature.

Sydney Such as?

Linda I know about Scott Fitzgerald for a start.

Kafka What about Scott Fitzgerald?

Linda He had a small p . . . Nothing.

She smiles. Kafka smiles back. She crosses her legs

Who's a clever girl then? (*Peal of laughter*)

Sydney He seems to like her.

Brod You mean she seems to like him. They always did. He has that kind of social ineptitude women mistake for sincerity.

Another peal of laughter

Sydney Linda. You're making a fool of yourself.

Linda No, I'm not. He's nice. You said he was nice. He is nice.

Brod Listen, you can do better than her. That's what fame means. Walk down the street and you'll be mobbed by autograph hunters, girls ready to do anything, anything just for your signature.

Kafka But what do I sign? My name. I hate my name. Fame is my name everywhere.

Brod That's right. Even on T-shirts. Worn by girls. Girls with no morals and degrees in European Literature. Girls who can mix Jane Austen with the latest developments in foreplay.

Linda How does he know?
Brod Because, *sister*, I'm famous too.
Kafka You? What for? Not your novels? They were terrible.
Sydney (*indicates the books*) For these. As you're famous so is he. His name
is synonymous with yours.
Kafka How? I'm not even synonymous with my own name.
Brod The ingratitude!
Linda I understand.
Sydney She doesn't.
Linda I wish I could make you happy.
Kafka There's only one thing that could make me happy. It's the look on
my father's face.
Linda Pride?
Kafka Disgust. "Look at this lot, Dad. I showed you."
Brod You want to be careful. He might turn up.

Kafka is instantly alarmed

Kafka How could he?
Linda You turned up.
Kafka I'm famous. I exist.
Sydney Your father's famous.
Kafka My *father*? My father ran a fancy goods store.
Sydney You were a minor civil servant.
Kafka My father was a bully. He made my life a misery. I blame him for
everything.
Brod So. Why do you think he's famous?
Kafka No. Tell me it's not true. He's buried and forgotten.

There is a ring at the bell

No. Max, what do I do? Hide me. Help me.

Linda answers the door

Linda (*off*) I'd forgotten I'd called you.

Linda enters

Don't be silly. It's not your father at all. It's a policeman.

*The Policeman, a burly figure in a raincoat, is also Kafka's father,
Hermann K. He enters and surveys the company without comment, then
circles the room to stand behind Kafka*

Policeman/Hermann K Hello, my son.

Kafka confronts his father as—

——*the* CURTAIN *falls*

ACT II

Kafka is alone on the stage, his novels and all the books about him in a pile in front of him. Very nervously, and with many precautions lest he be seen doing so he takes up one of the books. Before he can open it—

Linda enters, carrying two plates of food

Kafka hurriedly puts the book back

Linda (*showing Kafka one of the plates*) I've done you a hamburger.

Sydney enters R

Sydney He won't want that.
Linda Why?
Sydney He doesn't like meat.
Linda How do you know?
Sydney It's a matter of historical record.

Sydney exits L

Linda (*to Kafka, showing him another plate, on which is a piece of quiche*) Try this instead.
Kafka What's that?
Linda It's something unexpected I do with avocados. Tuck in.

Linda exits R

Sydney enters L

Sydney I imagine avocados must have been pretty thin on the ground in turn of the century Prague.
Kafka What do they taste like?
Sydney Soap.

Sydney exits R

Kafka looks at the plate with intense suspicion and puts it down. He starts to sneak another look at one of his books but is again interrupted, this time by Father

Father enters

Father This is him. He's got authority written all over him.
Kafka I want to ask you a question.
Father Here it comes.
Kafka Have you ever heard of someone called Kafka?
Father (*who has been about to answer, finds himself baffled*) Er . . .

Kafka It's supposed to be a household name.
Father You don't want the Prime Minister?
Kafka He was a Czech novelist. He died in 1924.
Father Six fours are twenty-four.

Kafka shakes his head

> I know the Prime Minister. I know the date and I can manage on the toilet with the bare minimum of assistance but if you're supposed to know the name of Czech novelists everybody's going to end up in a home. I had fifteen men under me.

Father exits

Kafka examines the quiche suspiciously. Smells it. Holds it up to the light. Looks for somewhere to hide it. Behind a cushion? In a vase? Finally, hearing someone coming, he makes a dash for the bookcase and slips it in there

> *Linda enters with a glass of milk, a napkin and a box of Black Magic chocolates. She spots the empty plate*

Linda I knew you'd enjoy that.
Kafka A novel experience. (*He checks the shelf*) I put it somewhere between Dostoevsky and Henry James.
Linda You know how to flatter a girl. Something else? A chocolate perhaps? I have a box of Black Magic I keep for emergencies.

Kafka shakes his head

Linda Your father ate the hamburger.
Kafka He would.
Linda I was hoping he'd do that trick of rummaging in his ears with a toothpick then using it to pick his teeth.
Kafka And did he?
Linda No. He has dentures now anyway.
Kafka That's an improvement.
Linda He thinks so. He passed them round for inspection.

Kafka groans

Kafka And he used to lecture me about *my* eating!
Linda The cheek. You're twice the man he is. Your constipation is in text books. (*Pause*) You've never had a stab at marriage then?
Kafka How could I? I was on such bad terms with my own body there was no room for a third party. You should see me in a bathing costume.
Linda It could be arranged.
Kafka It wasn't that I didn't like women. In fact I frequently got engaged to them. My fiancées tended to regard me as a species of invertebrate. Marriage was going to give me backbone.
Linda Clever, were they?
Kafka By and large. The last one, Dora, was very like you.
Linda I'm not clever.
Kafka But you are. You are a highly accomplished person.

Linda Me? What at?

Kafka How you enter a room, for instance, as a few moments ago you entered this room, bringing me a glass of milk. In the left hand you carry the milk. In the other hand a napkin and a box of chocolates. With an object in one hand and two objects in the other you have no hand to close the door, but no sooner does this dilemma present itself than you solve it, the right hand bringing the napkin and the box of chocolates over to the left side and tucking it between the upper part of the left arm and the rest of your body, which together co-operate to keep it clasped there, the linen and the chocolates sandwiched between the material of your dress and the arm, which is partly covered in the same material and partly . . . not. The right hand is now free so you place it on the doorknob and the fingers on that hand clasp the knob and pull it to. Free at last of the door, you take three steps into the room one leg effortlessly passing the other (your dress seems to consist of some light, woven fabric) until both legs come to a tentative halt at a point which (even with all these things on your mind, the milk, the chocolates, the moving legs) you have yet managed to find time to select as appropriate. Standing gently at rather than on this spot you lift the glass of milk towards me, managing as you do so to combine it with fetching the right hand over to the left side to take the napkin and the chocolates, now released by an agreement between your arm and your body. The two hands, one with milk, the other with the napkin and the chocolates, are now brought gently up towards me. I take the napkin and the milk but not the chocolates. To console the chocolates for this rebuff your left hand steals comfortingly into the box, selects one and carries it to your mouth. Finally, and still holding the chocolates, you sit down.

Linda I'm not surprised. I must have been exhausted. You forgot something.

Kafka Yes?

Linda When I was handing you the glass one of my fingers touched one of yours.

Kafka I hadn't forgotten. It was this finger. (*He holds up a finger*)

Linda And this.

She holds up her finger. It almost looks as if they might kiss, but they don't as Linda breaks away

   Brod and Sydney have entered

Sydney Was it always like this?

Brod No. I have to tell you. His girlfriends were women of great poise and intelligence or nubile young creatures of seventeen. In either category your wife hardly hits the bull's-eye.

Sydney This is intolerable. Linda.

Linda Excuse me. Sydney?

Sydney He should talk to his father.

Linda I don't believe he wants to, do you?

Kafka No.

Linda No.

Sydney Don't listen to her. She doesn't understand you. I've read your books. I admire you. I am a *fan*.

Kafka (*to Sydney*) You say you know me. I don't want to be known. (*To Linda*) He says he understands me: if he did understand me he'd understand that I don't want to be understood.

Linda Of course. I understand that. (*She doesn't*)

Sydney I read his books and this is the thanks I get.

Brod It's more thanks than I get and I practically wrote them.

Sydney I've had enough. I'm going to break this up.

Sydney exits

(*Calling as he goes*) Mr Kafka.

Kafka is instantly alarmed

Kafka Help me.

Linda I'm going to make a silly suggestion. Why don't you and your father just shake hands?

Kafka I can't.

Linda Why?

Kafka My hand is shaking.

Linda You're a grown man.

Kafka Not with my father around I'm not.

Hermann K enters, followed by Sydney

Hermann K Funny. They said I had a son here. They get into the dumbest places, sons. Some even get to the top of the tree. Only a good father tracks them down and brings them back to earth. I'm waiting.

Linda What for?

Hermann K I'm waiting for this son to fling his arms around me in heartfelt welcome, sink to his knees in abject remorse. I'm waiting for the brittle body and the hot consumptive breath. I'm braced for a kiss.

Kafka doesn't move, frozen in terror

Still as thin as a tram ticket. Did he eat?

Many of Hermann K's remarks are addressed to the audience. It's important that he should be on good terms with the audience, have a relationship with them, or he will just seem a bore and a bully. Perhaps it is that only the dead people can talk to the audience and are conscious of them, though Father talks to the audience too.

Linda Every scrap.

Hermann K He didn't put it down the toilet?

Linda No.

Hermann K That was his usual trick. Shepherd's pie floating in the toilet: show me a quicker way to break a mother's heart. So where? (*He looks round the room. Behind cushions, under the sofa, etc.*) My son had a problem with food. He didn't like it.

Kafka I ate nuts, raisins. Salad.

Linda Very healthy.

Hermann K For squirrels. I'm told he's done pretty well.

Sydney An understatement.

Brod No thanks to his father.

Hermann K I could debate that with you, Professor. My son is a near-delinquent. A spent condom.

Linda You've no business talking like that. This is a sensitive man.

Hermann K Lady. I'm the sensitive man. My son is about as sensitive as a gannet.

Sydney You're proud of him. You must be.

Hermann K Why? What's he done? Written a book or two. My father could lift a——

Hermann K
Brod } (*together*)—sack of potatoes in his teeth.

Brod He won't have read a word he's written.

Hermann K I tried to read one once. Flat as piss on a plate. When he makes *Reader's Digest*, then I'll read him.

Brod *Reader's Digest*! Last week I had a telegram from the *Oxford English Dictionary*. Your son is so famous that they named a word after him.

Hermann K What kind of word?

Brod An adjective. Kafka-esque.

Hermann K I never heard it. Has it caught on?

Brod Caught *on*? Your son now has adjectival status in Japanese.

Kafka Is this true?

Sydney Don't ask her, ask *me*. Of course it's true.

Brod They don't only write about you. They have to use you to write. Now you're a tool of the trade.

Kafka Thanks for nothing, Max.

Sydney Of course you're not the only one.

Kafka Proust?

Sydney Afraid so. Proustian.

Brod Kafka-esque is better.

Linda Look on the bright side. Most people have never heard of either of you.

Hermann K How's this word doing?

Sydney Famously. It crops up all the time. (*He picks up a newspaper*) Here we are. It's an article about Yves St. Laurent.

Kafka Who's he?

Linda A dress designer.

Kafka A dress designer?

Sydney "He is adept at coping with the Kafka-esque intrigues of high fashion."

Kafka High fashion? What's this high fashion? I never had anything to do with high fashion. What has Kafka to do with high fashion?

Brod Words don't always get used correctly. What matters is that they get used.

Hermann K Do we get a percentage?

Brod Words are free.

Hermann K If you make people a present of them, sure they are. My son has rights here. I told you this was a no-good friend. Your name exploited all over the world and what does he get you? Can you believe it? Nothing. Well, you'd better get out and stop them.

Brod How?

Hermann K The law. The authorities. Don't the police have some control over words?

Brod Yes. In Eastern Europe.

Kafka I don't understand it. "Kafka-esque intrigues of high fashion." I work in an insurance office. I have maybe three or four suits the whole of my life. I die a failure at the age of forty one. I get into the dictionary and suddenly I'm . . .

Sydney Hardy Amies.

Hermann K So, you should have listened to your father. Incidentally, does my son get to meet any of the models?

Brod turns away in despair

Some friend. He gives his name to a word and he can't even get a fuck out of it.

Linda (*to Kafka*) We didn't hear that, did we?

Sydney I'm sure your new friend has heard it before. He may even know what it means.

Hermann K I wouldn't bank on it. What would I have done with your chances. (*At the bookcase*) Edith Sitwell. You could have her. Evelyn Waugh. *Vile Bodies*. She sounds as if she knows how to please a man. I'm still waiting for this kiss.

Brod His name's an adjective in Japanese. Why should he kiss you?

Hermann K I was a simple man. I came from nothing. What was so wrong with my footsteps he didn't want to follow in them?

Kafka He sold *buttons*.

Hermann K Buttons, would you tell my son with the sick mind, that put him through college. I can see through him. You don't have to go to university to see through your own son . . . So, he wound up a writer. Did I stand in his way? Go, I said. Go. Walk in the high places of the earth. Be rich. Be famous. Only one day come home and lay a single flower on your father's grave.

Kafka I died before he did.

Hermann K He did. On purpose.

Brod I was at the funeral. You weren't upset. He wasn't upset at all.

Kafka That's right.

Hermann K How does he know? He was dead. He was where he always wanted to be, safely tucked up in his grave. He makes me sick standing there.

Linda And you make me sick, turning up and laying down the law. You . . . you great bladder of Czechoslovakian lard.

Sydney Linda.

Linda Why don't you and I go next door.
Kafka Yes.
Linda Then I can fix you something more to eat.
Kafka Maybe not.
Brod Old friend. Come with me into the garden.
Kafka Yes.
Brod Then I can tell you how big you are in New Zealand.
Kafka I don't want that either.
Hermann K Why don't you just talk to your father?
Kafka I want that least of all. Oh God!

Cornered, he finally makes a bolt for it into the kitchen

Linda (*smiling happily, and about to follow Kafka off*) Incidentally, what
was the woman's role in this household? What was his mother doing?
Brod Backing up his father.
Hermann K Naturally. We were a normal family.

Linda exits L

Brod exits into the garden

Sydney and Hermann K are alone

Hermann K So. You're a big fan of my son?
Sydney I'm writing an article about him if that's what you mean. I'm a fool.
I thought he'd be interested.
Hermann K I'm not interested either. These books, articles ... they're all
the same. For him whitewash, for me excrement.
Sydney Mine would have been different.
Hermann K Yes?
Sydney Having met your son I begin to think the books may have got him
wrong.
Hermann K That's interesting. In what way?
Sydney He's not quite the person I imagined him to be. I thought he was a
saint.
Hermann K You mean you don't any more?
Sydney No. I think posterity's got him wrong. He has faults like everybody
else.
Hermann K Ladies and gentlemen I have lain in my grave and dreamed of
this moment! Look ...
Sydney Sydney.
Hermann K Syd. I'm not an intellectual, I sold knicker elastic, so you'll
forgive me if I spell it out.
Sydney Do. I'm still trying to spell it out myself.
Hermann K Misjudge him, they misjudge me. If my son wasn't so good as
all the books make him out to be, and I wasn't so bad ... if we were, say,
more just a routine father and son then I wouldn't be the villain any more
and ...
Sydney And all the books would have to be re-written.

Hermann K And then people would see I was just an ordinary fellow and you'd be famous.

Sydney I'd be famous? How?

Hermann K A new view of Kafka, of course you would.

Sydney I hadn't thought of that. I could take time off from insurance.

Hermann K Time off? Time off? Fifty years of Kafka studies turned on their heads, you could travel the world, lecturing, giving talks *. . .*

Sydney People would know my name, students. I'd be famous! (*Pause*) But only if I'm right. Only if Kafka isn't a saint and you are just an ordinary father and son.

Hermann K You are right. And I'll prove it. Go fetch the little scallywag.

Sydney goes off, leaving Hermann alone

Father enters, with his walking frame, hat and coat on

Father Do you know what the latest is? Besides the date and the name of the Prime Minister they ask you the name of a leading Czech novelist.

Hermann K Else what?

Father They take you away.

Hermann K You can't be expected to know that.

Father Of course I know it. Franz Kafka.

Hermann K My son's even more famous than I thought! What about his father?

Father You're not supposed to know about his father?

Hermann K Of course. Everybody knows about Kafka's father.

Father Kafka wrote books.

Hermann K A book is a coffin and in it is your father's body.

Father I'd better go and swot it up. The buggers. Every time you're ready for the examination they change the syllabus!

Father exits

Hermann K Now. This is my chance to come over as a Normal Parent. (*He opens his arms, rehearsing his first embrace for his son*)

Kafka enters, pursued by Linda carrying food; they are followed on by Sydney

Linda You'll love it. It's kiwi fruit and satsuma segments. Didn't they have kiwi fruit in Prague?

Kafka No. Thank God.

Linda How did they manage?

Hermann K (*waiting for Kafka, arms outstretched*) Look at him. Don't you just love him. Come, give your Dad a kiss.

Kafka Who? Me? What is this?

Hermann K Baby. You've been rumbled.

Kafka Rumbled? What? Who? Don't touch me. What do you mean?

Hermann K What do I mean? I love the boy. Forget his faults, I love him.

Kafka Dad.

Linda It seems the affection is not returned.

Hermann K I know. I *know*. Lady, you are so right. That's what it seems.
But, as your clever little hubby has found out, things aren't always what
they seem. Until this moment everybody thought I hated my son. They
thought he hated me. (*He bursts out laughing*) The truth is, we're devoted
to each other.

He embraces the shrinking Kafka

Love me, dickhead. Do as I tell you.

Linda Leave him alone. Just because you're his father doesn't mean you can
kiss him. He hates his loved ones, we all know that. You don't believe
this?

Sydney Why not?

Linda You're pathetic.

Sydney All the evidence about Kafka's father comes from Kafka. The only
son who ever told the truth about his father was Jesus Christ—and there
are doubts about him.

Linda But this is a mean cheap person. Can't you *see*? He's a fraud.

Hermann K (*kissing Kafka*) Is this a fraud? Or this?

Kafka Father. You hate me, then all of a sudden you love me. What did I
do?

Hermann K Listen, you teetering column of urine, this clown is writing an
article about you.

Kafka I know.

Hermann K So. Don't you see? It's our big chance. We can be nice people. I
love this kid, this is someone really special.

Kafka Our big chance? Your big chance. I am nice people already.

Hermann K Yes. Thanks to me. Thanks to me being the shit. Bless him.

Sydney Look at that. Do you know what this is, Linda? That is a
breakthrough in Kafka studies.

Linda It looks more like somebody getting their arm twisted.

Sydney You used to be proud of me, Linda. You used to trust me.

Linda Sydney. I've talked to him.

Sydney I know. He's scarcely talked to anyone else. I've never had a look
in. I love him.

Hermann K So do I.

Kafka I don't want to have this conversation.

Linda You told me you couldn't stand one another. You blamed him for
everything.

Hermann K Lying.

Linda No.

Hermann K Tell her. Tell her it was all your fault. Or else.

Kafka Else what?

Hermann K Or else, you two-faced pisspot, I tell the world the one fact
biographers never know. I reveal the one statistic every man knows about
himself but which no book ever reveals. You see, sir, it's as I say, we're
just a normal father and son. My normal. (*He indicates about eight inches*)
Your normal. (*He indicates about three inches*)

Kafka No Dad. You wouldn't.

Hermann K No? There is one fact about my son and his . . . old man that has never got into print . . .
Linda Stand up to him. Come on.
Hermann K The long and the short of the matter is . . .

Brod enters

Kafka I was a terrible son. A dreadful son. A real father and mother of a son. And yet my father loved me.
Brod I don't believe what I'm hearing.
Hermann K Here's the real culprit. The original biographer. The man who led posterity up the garden path in the first place.
Kafka Max. Help me.
Brod Suddenly I'm forgiven. So what's the problem?
Hermann K You're at it again. The same old game. Coming between a father and son. Well, not any more. Now for the first time the truth is going on record. Say it again, my son.
Kafka My father loved me. It was all my fault.
Brod Brilliant. And your lips didn't even move. What's he got on you this time?
Kafka Nothing. Honestly.
Brod Listen. Max is back. We're friends again. The old team. Tell this gorilla to get lost.
Kafka No, Max.
Brod Are you saying you lied to me?
Kafka Yes.
Linda And you lied to me?
Kafka I lied to everybody.
Brod Why?
Sydney Because he was a writer. Writers do lie. They exaggerate because they always think they're the injured party. That's one of the things you learn in insurance: the injured party always exaggerates.
Hermann K Yes. You boys of art, you're all the same. I want to hear it again. How much did I love you? (*Indicating three inches*) A little. (*Indicating eight inches*) Or a lot.
Kafka I can't tell you how much.
Brod I'm nauseated.
Linda You're hiding something?
Kafka No. It's just that there were faults on both sides.
Hermann K We sparred a little, sure, but who doesn't?
Brod Sparred? "Eat your meat or I'll get a long spoon and cram it down your throat like they do in prisons."
Hermann K That's me. And you say I was wrong. Dr Spock says I was wrong. The *Cambridge History of Literature* says I was wrong. Does he say I was wrong?
Kafka You were right, Father. Parents love their children so they make them eat.
Hermann K True?
Linda I don't know. We have no children.

Hermann K So what do you know about anything?
Brod You tried to stop him writing. You even hid his ink.
Hermann K What time was it?
Kafka Three in the morning.
Hermann K What time did you have to go to work?
Kafka Seven. You were right. A boy needs sleep.
Brod He tried to stop you writing altogether.
Hermann K Of course I did. That's how clever I was. If I'd said "Stick to the writing" he would probably have ended up a chartered accountant. Hermann Kafka didn't fall off the Christmas tree yesterday. Right, my son?

Kafka nods unhappily

Kiss? Mmm. Yours a little kiss. Mine a big kiss.
Linda I think you might have told me. I told you about Sydney.
Sydney What?
Brod I'm the one he should have told. I wrote his biography. I gave him to the world. I'm nauseated.
Sydney What about me?
Linda I told him I wasn't very happy.
Sydney That's you. You said you'd told him about me.
Kafka How long do I have to keep up this charade?
Hermann K Until people start liking me more than they like you. Until they realize what a handful you were. Until I get into the books in a proper light and posterity has finally got to hand it to me, that's how long.
Kafka It will never happen.
Hermann K So should I tell them your little secret . . .
Kafka No.
Hermann K Then cuddle me, you soiled bandage. Snuggle up.
Kafka *Cuddle* you. I'm Kafka. I never cuddled anyone in my life.
Hermann K So you've just made a breakthrough. And not gingerly. If there's one thing I can't stand it's gingerly cuddling. Hey, just look at this boy. Someone take a picture.
Brod I am nauseated by this. Sick to my scrotum. The shrinking hypocrisy of it. Seen here embracing his son, one of the most notorious shits in literary history.
Hermann K (*gleefully*) I *know.*
Brod What is it you're hiding?
Kafka *Nothing*, honestly.
Hermann K Go into the garden, son. Get some fresh air. But remember, I love you.

Brod is about to follow

No. Sorry. I think my son would prefer to be alone, wouldn't you, son?
Kafka Yes, father.

He exits

Brod You make me sick.
Hermann K I know.

Brod exits

Hermann K So I'm going to come well out of this article?
Sydney An ordinary fellow.
Hermann K Well, don't think I'm not grateful. Anything you want in the
  soft-furnishing line, high-quality fancy goods, you only have to ask.
  Curtaining materials, rufflette, those little mats you put under glasses to
  stop them making a nasty ring on a nice polished table . . . A man wants to
  show his gratitude, exonerated after all these years. I feel sorry for my
  son, naturally, pushed off his pedestal, but the truth had to come out.
Sydney You were found guilty on false evidence.
Hermann K I was. Trial. I never had a trial. This is the joke: my son writes a
  book about someone who's had up for a crime he didn't commit and
  everybody thinks the book's about him. It's not. It's about me. In fact, if I
  weren't so fond of my son I'd say he's the one who should be put on trial.
Linda In what way?
Hermann K No, no. Forget I said it. Fundamentally this is a good boy.
Linda Try him for what?
Hermann K Perjury. Bearing false witness against his father.
Sydney It isn't only that. There are other charges. Other questions.
Linda But you admired him.
Sydney I did. I do . . . though he's not the man I thought he was. Still there's
  no question of you trying him: you're his father.
Hermann K You're in insurance. Investigation and assessment, it's right up
  your street.
Linda There's a difference between a man's reputation and a scratch on the
  bodywork. Sydney's no judge. He's . . .
Sydney What?
Linda He's nobody.
Sydney I married you.
Linda That proves it, probably.
Sydney Well, I may be a nobody, Linda, but what I am is a reader. And
  writers are tried by readers every time they open their books. Fetch him.
  He trusts you.

*Sydney places the walking frame to act as a makeshift dock and draws the
curtains*

The stage darkens

Linda Sydney. This is persecution.
Sydney No, it's not. It's biography.
Brod My biography never put him in the dock.
Sydney I know. That's what was wrong with it.

Linda exits

After a moment, Kafka creeps in. He sees the dock waiting

Kafka Max, Father . . .
Hermann K Don't look at me.
Kafka What have I done?
Sydney (*taking the frame and putting it in front of Kafka*) You are famous. Fame is a continuing offence. It leaves you open to trial at any time.
Kafka But I didn't want fame.
Brod I know. It's all my fault. But I bet you still expect me to defend you.
Linda Why don't I defend you?
Sydney You?
Kafka How? You know nothing about me.
Linda I like you. Nobody else seems to.
Sydney I do, given the chance.
Linda Then why the trial?
Sydney I just want to cut him down to size. If I do that I might make my name. Don't you want me to make my name?
Linda No. Not at the expense of his.
Sydney Do you, Sydney, take this bottle of hydrochloric acid, Linda, to be your lawful wedded wife? Splendid. Would you, Linda, take your stiletto heel and force it up the groom's nose. Excellent. I now pronounce you man and wife. *All right.* You defend. I prosecute, and we'll see who wins. Right?
Linda Right.
Kafka (*in the middle*) Oh dear.
Sydney Very well. Let's kick off with this question of your name. While every other writer one can think of wants to make his name, you want to unmake yours. So you unravel your name until there's only one letter left: K. You sign your letters K, you refer to yourself as K. What was it you disliked about Kafka?
Linda What is it you disliked about Sydney?
Sydney I dislike Sydney because it carries within it the unhatched threat of Syd. And if you can't do any better than that I'd leave it to him (*he indicates Brod*). What was it you disliked about Kafka?
Kafka It means jackdaw. A thief. It also means me.
Sydney Can I suggest another reason? The name Kafka. Treat it like an equation in algebra. Take the F to one side of the equation and what are we left with? F equals Kaka. Franz is shit. Is that why you disliked it?
Linda Better than Syd.
Brod And T. S. Eliot is an anagram of toilets so does that make him a closet? This isn't biography. It's not even literary criticism. It's the only thing the English are good at . . . crossword puzzles. He denies it. He denies everything.
Kafka F equals Kaka. Truthfully, it hadn't occurred to me, but now you point it out it's not a bad idea.
Brod What do you do with this man?
Kafka My name, it was like a tin can tied to the tail of a cat, I wanted rid of it.
Sydney Quite, and though you get the credit for trying to lose your name,

you never do lose it. You make it famous. And the person who does lose his name gets no credit for it at all.

Hermann K Who was that?

Sydney You.

Hermann K Me? Exactly! Was it?

Sydney Yes.

Brod Him?

Hermann K That's right. In Prague in 1919 stop any passing housewife and say Kafka and she'd direct you to my shop by the Town Hall. Cheerful service, high-quality goods, value for money, Kafka's is the place.

Sydney And what happens if you say you're Kafka now?

Hermann K "You Kafka?" people say. "Kafka didn't have a moustache for a start. Kafka is the skinny guy with the big ears on the back of the Penguins." Suddenly I don't exist. So, Mr Name-Dropper. I'm the one who loses his name. Gets de-nominated. Mr Hermann Kafka. Only I didn't lose it. It was taken. By my son.

Brod All sons take their father's name.

Linda Not only sons. (*To Sydney*) You took my name. When I married you.

Sydney And?

Linda Why is it when a woman gets married we say she takes her husband's name? What we mean is he takes hers. Takes it and buries it.

Hermann K All right, so you lose your name too, dear. The point the gentleman is making, precious, is that the one person who didn't lose his name is the person who claimed to want to lose it, and the person who got the credit for losing it: my son.

Linda And whose fault is that? (*She points at Brod*)

Brod He was in two minds. He was always in two minds. I did him a good turn.

Sydney I've never understood that.

Brod It's called friendship.

Sydney Did he ever do you a good turn?

Kafka I made him famous.

Sydney But that's not a good turn, is it? When Kafka was alive, of the two of you who is the better known?

Brod I'd published several novels. He'd published almost nothing. I was a poet, a critic. Me, no question. With a comparable reputation in Czechoslovakia today I'd probably be a well-known dissident.

Sydney And what was Kafka when you knew him?

Brod A friend of Max Brod.

Sydney Whereas today . . .

Brod It's the other way round.

Linda That's nothing to be ashamed of. The great man's friend. That's all a woman gets. That's all a wife would have got.

Brod But I wasn't his wife. I was someone in my own right.

Kafka And my best friend. Rather nice I should have thought.

Brod If not to exist is nice. And since you do think not existing is nice, maybe it is.

Kafka Don't you exist?

Brod Not any more. I go on publishing novels after you die, notching up steady sales. Only then I start publishing yours. Result: as soon as they read yours they don't want to know about mine. (*He takes out some clippings*) This is my last novel. It was about the Arab–Israeli War. This reviewer found in it "a trace of Kafka's imagery but" (here it comes) "none of that simple fascinating prose style that makes Kafka readable." You readable! You may have been a genius, but you were never readable. You finished me as a novelist. All I could do was go round lecturing about the Kafka I knew. "Kafka as I remembered him." Or Kafka as I remembered remembering him. What you were actually like I'd forgotten till now. I had no life of my own any more.

Linda You *were* his wife.

Brod No. I was his widow.

Linda Even better.

Sydney Would you say your friend was good-looking?

Brod Yes. Yes, I would.

Kafka No.

Hermann K There has to be something about him, hasn't there? He's my son.

Sydney You think he's good-looking, don't you?

Linda In comparison w—— yes.

Kafka My body wasn't satisfactory. I couldn't bear to look at it.

Sydney Your diaries show you looked at it all the time.

Kafka Only in disgust.

Sydney Do you grumble about your physique to your friend here?

Brod Does he ever!

Kafka Do I? I don't remember.

Brod When don't you? Every imperfection of the body tormented you. Constipation, a toe that wasn't properly formed, even dandruff. Toes and dandruff. I wished I'd had your problems.

Kafka Why?

Brod Why? You prick in a bottle. You turd in a hat. *Why*? Did you never look at me? My spine was twisted. You're complaining to me about dandruff. I was a *hunchback*.

Linda He's not a hunchback now.

Brod There's not much to be said for death, but it is the end of disability.

Sydney Your sensitive friend.

Linda Say something. Defend yourself.

Kafka What for? Nobody can reproach me with failings for which I have not reproached myself. List my shortcomings now, I listed them all half a century ago. Find fault with me now, what is the evidence: my own fault finding then. I stand here self-examined, self-confessed and self-convicted.

Hermann K Self, self, self.

Kafka Nobody ever believed what I said about myself. When I said I exaggerated they thought I was exaggerating. When I said I lied, they thought I lied. I said I was an agent of the devil, they thought this meant I was a servant of God. When I said they must not believe me, they did not

believe me. But now you believe me. Only now when at last you find I was
telling the truth about myself you call me a liar.

Linda I don't think you're a liar.

Kafka But you'd agree I was a terrible human being?

Linda No. Pretty average, if you ask me.

Brod Average? Kafka is average?

Sydney And now as in some Czech village wooing Kafka pauses with his
rucksack at the garden gate, asks for a lemonade and our brisk Shavian
heroine reads him a lesson on life and generally pulling his socks up.

Linda When I first saw you I thought here's somebody different. I can talk
to this man. And what's more peculiar he listens. He notices. I also
thought what nice hands.

Kafka And now?

Linda I still like your hands.

Kafka But I'm a terrible human being.

Linda No.

Kafka No?

Linda No. You're a man, that's all.

Sydney Oh no.

All the men except Kafka groan

Kafka Not much of a man.

Linda Every inch.

Hermann K sniggers

Kafka Dad.

Linda You're a man, because, although you despair, at the same time like
all men you believe your despair is important. You think you're insignificant but your insignificance is not insignificant. Oh no.

Kafka That's because I'm a writer.

Linda No. It's because you are a man. Whatever happens or doesn't happen
to you matters. You may not want the world to think you're somebody,
provided it recognizes you are nobody.

Kafka But I am nobody.

Linda Why *tell* us? Women can be nobodies all the time and who cares? All
these letters to your girlfriends ... Letters to Milena, letters to Felice.
Saved. Published. Where are their letters to you? Lost. Thrown away.
That's a man.

Kafka I was born a man.

Linda What excuse is that? You changed into a beetle, a dog, an ape, the
one thing you never transformed yourself into was the lowliest creature of
all ... a woman.

Sydney Good try, but you're wrong. One of the last stories he wrote is
about a female, Josephina, a singing mouse.

Kafka You're defending me now.

Brod Against her? Of course he is. We have to stick together. Anyway, why
save your girlfriends' letters? Are they literature?

Hermann K Women.

Linda Are you disappointed in me?

Kafka No. I always expect to be disappointed. If I'm not disappointed, then I'm disappointed.

Linda I always feel I want to mother him.

Kafka No. Once was enough.

Kafka tries to leave the dock

Sydney One last point. You never saw fascism, communism, the totalitarian state.

Kafka No. By that time I was safely tucked up in my grave.

Sydney Your work suggests you would not have been happy under such regimes.

Kafka Does it? I can't say.

Sydney Oh, I think so. Your reputation today, at least among those who know your name but haven't read you (which is the measure of literary reputation after all) ... your reputation stands high as a man who protested (though don't ask in what respect precisely), a man who shook his fist (helplessly, no doubt) against authority, officialdom, the law. You were, if not an enemy of the state, a friend of the enemies of the state. Is that reputation justified, do you think?

Kafka I have told you. Any reputation is a burden.

Sydney Where could you have shed that burden? Where would you be happiest?

Kafka It's not a place that exists in the world.

Sydney Why?

Kafka It would be a place where I am read only by vermin, the outcasts of the community, the convicts and exiles. I would be read by untouchables, furnacemen, sweepers of roads. Furtively, with discretion and behind locked doors. It would be a place where I am read, but not named, known but not spoken of, studied but not taught. That would be my ideal state.

Sydney There is a place like that.

Kafka Where? It must be wonderful. I'd like to live there.

Sydney You did. It's called Prague. (*He takes the frame away, and puts it offstage*)

Kafka Is the trial over?

Sydney For the time being. (*He takes his manuscript*) The process goes on, of course, I've no need to tell you that. Articles, books ... every day is——

Kafka —a day of judgement. I know.

All clear, leaving Hermann K alone on the stage as Father comes in, either with his frame, or a makeshift version of it, like a chair

Father Don't go. I want you to test me. Ask me any question you want about this Czech novelist *or* his father. I think you'll find it's all at my fingertips.

Hermann K What was his father like?

Father Dreadful. And a shocking bully. Made his son's life a misery. The root of all the trouble. Is that right? It is. Ten out of ten. Father goes to the top of the class. Now at last I can reveal the name of the Prime Minister . . .

Hermann K Sorry.

Father What?

Hermann K You're wrong.

Father I never am. I looked in all the books.

Hermann K The books are wrong. Kafka's father was a normal parent.

Father A normal parent? How am I expected to remember a normal parent: I'm a normal parent. Nobody remembers me.

Hermann K He was an average father.

Father But the world's full of average fathers. Average fathers are two a penny. An average father? I'm never going to remember that.

Father goes off leaving Hermann K pensive

Hermann K Hermann Kafka, you want your head examining. You're trying to come over as a nice parent and get into all the books. What for? Nice parents don't get into the books. With nice parents there are no books.

Kafka enters

Listen, son. A change of plan. I want you to do as I tell you.

Kafka Haven't you finished torturing me? You've destroyed my character, lost me my best friend . . .

Hermann K And now I'm going to do you a good turn.

Kafka No, please. Not that. Not a good turn.

Hermann K Can I have your attention please? That's everybody.

Father returns to the stage

No, not you.

Father You said everybody.

Hermann K I mean everybody who matters.

Father exits again as Linda, Sydney and Brod enter

Linda Do we matter?

Sydney (*with his manuscript*) We certainly do. This isn't just an article, Linda. It's going to be a book. And when it's finished I shall dedicate it to you.

Linda Yes? To the wall on which I bounced my ball. To the tree against which I cocked my leg.

Sydney Linda. I shan't be an insurance man any more. I shall be a literary figure. You'll be the wife of a famous man.

Hermann K (*gleefully*) Oh no she won't.

Sydney Well, not famous exactly, but . . .

Hermann K Not famous *at all*. Because there isn't going to be an article. There isn't going to be a book.

Sydney But ... why not?

Hermann K Because I've decided to come clean. I'm every bit as bad as the books make me out. Worse.

Sydney I don't understand.

Hermann K You're an insurance man. You must be familiar with false claims. This was a false claim. Both parties were lying.

Kafka Father.

Hermann K Shut your face, you wet dishcloth.

Linda I knew you were lying.

Sydney But why deceive me?

Hermann K I'm human. Just. I wanted to be liked.

Linda (*to Hermann K*) But why did you lie?

Hermann K Blackmail.

Kafka Dad!

Hermann K Don't you Dad me, you dismal Jimmy. Do you want to know how I made him toe the line?

Kafka You promised!

Hermann K You know me: I'm your terrible father. When did I ever keep a promise? Besides, I owe it to posterity. I don't know how to put this delicately ...

Brod It's never been a problem before.

Kafka puts his hands over his ears

Hermann K The long and short of it is: my son is ashamed of his old man.

Brod We know that. That's what all the books say, starting with mine.

Hermann K No, not me. He's ashamed of his old man.

Kafka Don't listen. Please don't listen.

Hermann K Putting it bluntly: his old man doesn't compare with his old man's old man. His. Mine. (*He makes an unequivocal gesture*)

Sydney But I know that. Everyone knows that.

Linda Even I know that.

Kafka You? How?

Sydney (*finding the book*) *Dreams, Life and Literature*. A study of Kafka by Hall and Lind, University Press, North Carolina.

Linda So you see, your private parts have long been public property.

Kafka He's won again. When will it ever stop?

Hermann K Stop? Stop? Mr World Famous Writer with the Small Dick, it won't ever stop. Literature goes on. You are one of its big heroes and I am one of its small villains.

Linda I'm a little confused.

Brod That's nothing fresh.

Linda You didn't like your son?

Hermann K No.

Linda But then you said you did.

Hermann K Yes.

Linda And now you say you didn't.

Hermann K Yes.

Linda Sydney. (*Pause*) Is that what they mean by Kafka-esque?

Hermann K I thought I wanted to be a good father.

Linda Yes.

Hermann K Now I don't.

Linda Why?

Hermann K Because, *snowdrop*, a good father is a father you forget.

Brod You had a good father. You haven't forgotten him.

Hermann K I have.

Brod But he could ...

Linda   ⎫ (*together*) ... lift a sack of potatoes with his teeth.
Hermann K ⎭

Hermann K Yes. But that's *all* I can remember about him. Whereas bad fathers are never forgotten. They jump out of the wardrobe. They hide under the bed. They come on as policemen. Sons never get rid of them. So long as my son's famous, I'm famous. I figure in all the biographies, I get invited to all the parties. I'm a bad father, so I'm in the text.

Brod Same old Hermann.

Hermann K Anyway I couldn't change things now. My accountant would never forgive me.

Herman K goes

Father enters, just missing Hermann K

Father Has he gone? Damn. I was wanting to bring him abreast of the latest turnaround in Kafka studies. Whereas we have all been brought up to suppose that Kafka and his father were at daggers drawn, recent research has revealed that they both got on famously.

Brod Wrong.

Father You can't have me taken away when I'm in touch with the latest developments in Kafka studies. What did you say?

Linda You're wrong.

Father No. No. You're trying to confuse me. They were like you and me — friends.

Sydney No, Dad. They couldn't stand one another.

Father I give up. Put me away. My limited studies of Kafka have convinced me that being a vegetable is not without its attractions.

He retires

Kafka Thank God I was never a father. It's the one achievement nobody can take away.

Brod You don't need to have children in order to be a father. You were so dedicated to writing, so set on expressing yourself even if it killed you, which it eventually did, that, like the best and worst of fathers you have been an example and a reproach to writers ever since. (*Meaning Sydney*) Take him. He loves you. He hates you. So do I.

Linda You're not sorry?

Brod How should I be sorry? If I hadn't been Kafka's friend I wouldn't have been in the play.

Sydney If you hadn't been Kafka's friend there would have been no play. There would have been no Kafka.

Kafka is about to speak

Brod Now don't say it.

Kafka puts his hand on Brod's shoulder and smiles

Be content. We will meet at that posthumous cocktail party, posterity.

Brod goes

Kafka Shall we see you there?
Linda Who says we'll be invited?
Sydney (*picking up the manuscript*) This is our invitation.
Linda Is it? Fifteen thousand books and articles about Kafka. What's one more? Poor Sydney. Anyway you hate parties.
Sydney This one might have been different.
Linda That's what one always thinks, every, every time.
Kafka You are so like Dora.
Linda Enjoy yourself. Be miserable.
Kafka I will. You know me.

They touch fingers as they touched before

Kafka vanishes

Sydney You see, try as we will, we can never quite touch Kafka. He always eludes us. We never do know him.
Linda I know him better than you.
Sydney Really? So what's this? (*He takes the quiche out of the bookcase*)
Linda (*hurt*) His lunch. My quiche. Oh, Sydney.
Sydney (*consoling her*) I'll eat it.

They share it

Linda Who was Dora?
Sydney His last girlfriend. The only one who made him happy. She got him to eat, wrap up warm. Nursed him, I suppose. She wasn't interested in his work at all. When he told her to burn some of it, she did. (*Pause*) You'd better burn this, I suppose.
Linda Are you sure?
Sydney Yes.

She gathers it up briskly and is going

Wait. What do you think?
Linda Since when does it matter what I think? (*She is going again*)
Sydney Linda. Do *you* think I should burn it?
Linda How do I know? I haven't read it.
Sydney Will you read it?
Linda That depends. I may not have time. Now Father's off our hands I'm going back to nursing. (*Pause*) Anyway I couldn't have burned it.

Sydney is touched. She hands back the manuscript

We're in a smokeless zone.

Sydney You're not stupid.

Linda No. After all, I know that Auden never wore underpants and Mr Right for E. M. Forster was an Egyptian tramdriver. Only some day I'll learn the bits in between.

Sydney (*a cry of despair*) Oh Linda. There's no need. This is England. In England facts like that pass for culture. Gossip is the acceptable face of intellect.

Linda What I don't understand, she said, like the secretary in the detective story when the loose ends are being tied up, what I still don't understand is why people are so interested in a writer's life in the first place.

Sydney You like fairy stories.

Linda If they have happy endings.

Sydney This one does, every, every, time. We are reading a book. A novel, say, or a book of short stories. It interests us because it is new, because it is ... novel, so we read on. And yet in what we call our heart of hearts (which is the part that is heartless) we know that like children we prefer the familiar stories, the tales we have been told before. And there is one story we never fail to like because it is always the same. The myth of the artist's life. How one struggled for years against poverty and indifference only to die and find himself famous. Another is a prodigy finding his way straight to the public's heart to be loved and celebrated while still young, but paying the price by dying and being forgotten. Or just dying.

During the following the Lights concentrate on Sydney and music starts in the distance

This one is a hermit, that one a hellraiser but the myth can accommodate them all, no variation on it but it is familiar even to someone who has never read a book. He plunges from a bridge and she hits the bottle. Both of them *paid*. That is the myth. Art is not a gift, it is a transaction, and somewhere an account has to be settled. It may be in the gas oven, in front of a train or even at the altar but on this side of the grave or that settled it must be. We like to be told, you see, that you can't win. We prefer artists to die poor and forgotten, like Rembrandt, Mozart or Beethoven, none of whom did, quite. One reason why Kafka is so celebrated is because his life conforms in every particular to what we have convinced ourselves an artist's life should be. Destined to write he dispenses with love, with fame and finally with life itself so that it seems at the last he has utterly failed. But we know that in the fairy story this is what always happens to the hero just before his ultimate triumph. It is not the end.

Sydney and Linda go

As the Lights come up we are in Heaven, which is a big party going on offstage

Kafka enters through the french windows, which have become the Pearly Gates, and finds the Recording Angel, played by Brod

Kafka I don't know what I'm doing here. I shouldn't be in Heaven.

Angel Good. That proves you're in the right place.

Kafka I don't feel I deserve it.

Angel That proves you do. The worse you feel, the better you are, that's the celestial construct.

Kafka Will I be allowed to be as despairing here as I was on earth?

Angel You can be as gloomy as you like so long as it makes you happy. Look at Ibsen. He can just about manage a smile for Strindberg but nobody else. Now who don't you know? The gentleman over there with the shocking beard, that's Dostoevsky. Who's he talking to? Oh. Noël Coward! They've got a lot of ground to cover. There's Wittgenstein and Betty Hutton. Got it together at last! There's Proust (Hi, Marcel!) trying to con one of the waiters into making him a cup of tea so that he can do his act. (Kissy kissy!) Oh, and there's the Virgin Mary.

Kafka She looks sad.

Angel She's never got over not having grandchildren. I say to her, well, look on the bright side. What about Gothic architecture? With two thousand years of Christianity to your credit what are grandchildren? But, as she said to me in a moment of confidence, "You can't knit bootees for the Nicene Creed."

Kafka Are there Jews here?

Angel *Mais oui!* In droves.

Kafka And there's no quota?

Angel Not officially. Though God is quite keen on them, naturally.

Kafka I was fond of animals. Are they here?

Angel Sorry, love. No animals. Well, they don't have a moral life.

Kafka No mice, beetles or birds?

Angel No. But if St Francis of Assisi can get used to it, I'm sure you can. You didn't really like them anyway. They were only metaphors. No metaphors here. No allegory. And nobody says "hopefully" or "at the end of the day" or "at this moment in time". We're in a presence of God situation here, you see. Talk of the Devil here comes God.

God (who is, of course, Hermann K) enters

God My son!

Kafka Who are you?

God Well, I'm all sorts of things. The BBC, Harrods. The *Oxford English Dictionary*. The Queen. The Ordnance Survey Map. Anything with a bit of authority really.

Kafka You're my father.

God Of course. What did you expect? Enjoying yourself?

Kafka No. It's like a terrible party.

God It is a party. And I'm the Host. (*He should plainly be itching to dance, looking over his son's shoulder and waving at other (invisible) guests, all the time he's talking*) There's Gandhi. Go easy on the cheese straws, Mahatma! You're going to have to watch that waistline! Can you dance?

Kafka No.

God I can. Mind you, I can do everything. Nuclear physics, the samba . . . it's all one to me.

Kafka Oh God.

God Yes? Come on. Just be happy you're invited. I bet you never thought you'd see Leonard Woolf doing the cha-cha.

Sydney crosses

Sydney I'm not doing the cha-cha. It's Virginia. She's just put a hot cocktail sausage down my neck.

God (*calling after them*) You could have fooled me, Len. He couldn't of course. I know it all.

Kafka Father. Did you ever get round to reading my books?

God Are you still on about that? No, of course not. No fiction here anyway. No writing. No literature. No art. No need. After all what were they? Echoes, imitations. This is the real thing. Son. Try not to disappoint me this time. And there's no shortage of time. We're here for ever, you and me.

Kafka Yes, Father.

God Listen, unless I'm very much mistaken (and that's a theological nonsense) that sounds to me like the rumba and I've promised it to Nurse Cavell.

Linda comes on in a nurse's costume but with a Carmen Miranda headgear

Kafka Nurse Cavell didn't look like Carmen Miranda.

God I know. Why do you think they shot her?

Father has come on playing the maracas

And now, as the magic fingers of Bertrand Russell beat out a mad mazurka on the maracas, I must go and move in my well-known mysterious way. *Ciao*, son.

Kafka *Ciao*, Father.

The music swells as God and Carmen Miranda dance

The stage is suddenly dark and Kafka comes forward

I'll tell you something. Heaven is going to be hell.

CURTAIN

FURNITURE AND PROPERTY LIST

ACT I

SCENE 1

On stage: Chair

SCENE 2

(See directions on page 4)

On stage: Bookcase. *On shelves:* various books including Penguin editions of Kafka's work, biographies etc.
Sofa. *On it:* cushions, books
Armchair
Manuscript and books for **Sydney**

Off stage: Table **(Linda)**

Personal: **Brod:** large, Homburg hat concealing a tortoise
Father: Zimmer frame (used throughout), small attaché case

ACT II

Off stage: Plate of quiche, plate with hamburger **(Linda)**
Glass of milk, napkins, box of Black Magic chocolates **(Linda)**
Dish of kiwi fruit and satsuma segments **(Linda)**
Manuscript **(Sydney)**

Personal: **Brod:** Newspaper clippings

During black-out on page 47

Strike: All furniture and properties

Off stage: Maracas **(Father)**

LIGHTING PLOT

ACT I, SCENE 1

To open: Full general lighting

Cue 1   **Brod:** "Come to bed."   (Page 4)
           Start fade to Black-out

ACT I, SCENE 2

To open: Full general lighting

No cues

ACT II

To open: Full general lighting

Cue 2   **Sydney** draws the curtains   (Page 37)
           Lights dim

Cue 3   **Sydney:** "Or just dying."   (Page 47)
           Start fade to spot on **Sydney**

Cue 4   **Sydney** and **Linda** go   (Page 47)
           Black-out

Cue 5   When ready   (Page 47)
           Bring up full general lighting

Cue 6   As God and Carmen Miranda dance   (Page 49)
           Snap to downstage spot for **Kafka**

EFFECTS PLOT

ACT I

ACT II

*Optional

MADE AND PRINTED IN GREAT BRITAIN BY
LATIMER TREND & COMPANY LTD PLYMOUTH

MADE IN ENGLAND